Cool STEAM Careers

Medical Illustrator

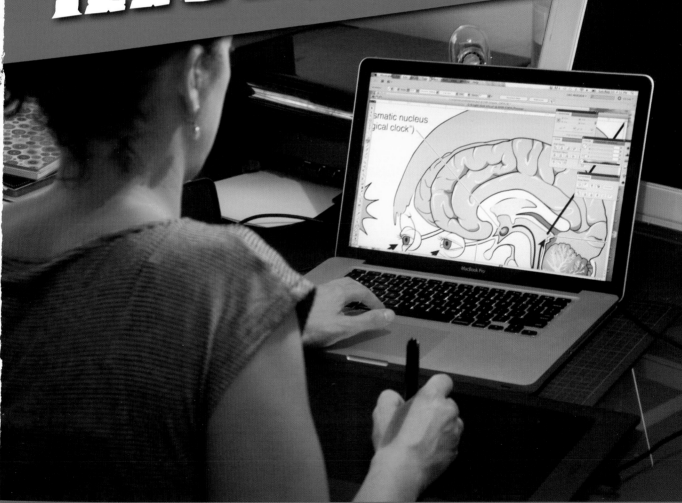

NEL YOMTOV

Published in the United States of America by Cherry Lake Publishing
Ann Arbor, Michigan
www.cherrylakepublishing.com

Content Adviser: John Megahan, Senior Biological Illustrator, University of Michigan Museum of Zoology, Ann Arbor, Michigan.
Reading Adviser: Marla Conn, ReadAbility, Inc.

Photo Credits: ©Joel Beals, Artist=Patricia Ferrer Beals, cover, 1, 18; ©BlueRingMedia/Shutterstock Images, 5; ©Dorling Kindersley/Thinkstock, 6; ©sam100/Shutterstock Images, 9; ©4X-image/Thinkstock, 11; ©Mushakesa/Shutterstock Images, 12; ©Lightspring/Shutterstock Images, 15; ©Bork/Shutterstock Images, 17; ©DJTaylor/CanStockPhoto, 21; ©Linda Huang/"Histology Demo" Artist=Gretchen Kai Halpert. Physician=I-Rue Lai M.D, PhD Department of Anatomy and Cell Biology,NTU, 22; ©Ron Faris/"At Scope" Artist=Gretchen Kai Halpert, 25; ©CandyBox Images/Shutterstock Images, 26; ©Mopic/Shutterstock Images, 27; ©wavebreakmedia/Shutterstock Images, 28

Library of Congress Cataloging-in-Publication Data

Yomtov, Nelson, author.
Medical illustrator / Nel Yomtov.
     pages cm. — (Cool STEAM Careers)
 Summary: "Readers will learn what it takes to succeed as a medical illustrator. The book also explains the necessary educational steps, useful character traits, and daily job tasks related to this career, in the framework of the STEAM (Science, Technology, Engineering, Art, and Math) movement. Photos, a glossary, and additional resources are included."— Provided by publisher.
 Audience: Ages 8-12.
 Audience: Grades 4 to 6.
 Includes bibliographical references and index.
 ISBN 978-1-63362-003-2 (hardcover) — ISBN 978-1-63362-042-1 (pbk.) — ISBN 978-1-63362-081-0 (pdf) — ISBN 978-1-63362-120-6 (ebook) 1. Medical illustrators—Juvenile literature. 2. Medical illustration—Vocational guidance—Juvenile literature. 3. Biological illustration—Juvenile literature. I. Title.

R836.Y66 2014
610.222023—dc23   2014031657

Cherry Lake Publishing would like to acknowledge the work of
The Partnership for 21st Century Skills. Please visit www.p21.org
for more information.

Printed in the United States of America
Corporate Graphics

ABOUT THE AUTHOR

Nel Yomtov is an award-winning author of nonfiction books and graphic novels for young readers. He lives in the New York City area.

TABLE OF CONTENTS

STEAM is the acronym for Science, Technology, Engineering, Arts, and Mathematics. In this book, you will read about how each of these study areas is connected to a career in medical illustration.

CHAPTER 1

PICTURE THIS!

Carlos and his father were sitting in their living room watching television one night. They were deeply absorbed in a program about the **circulatory system** of the human body. The program featured many illustrations and **animations** that showed how blood travels through the body.

"Those drawings and cartoons are really cool, Dad," Carlos said. "They show so much detail."

"Maybe even more than a photograph," replied his dad. "Illustrations can show the **anatomy** of humans,

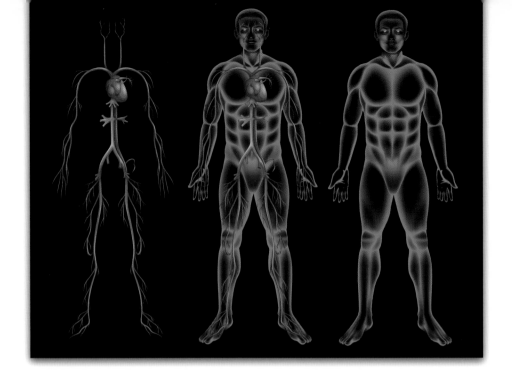

Medical illustrators share information through their drawings.

animals, and plants, and explain surgical procedures and lots more."

"The drawings help me understand what's going on," Carlos said. "I wonder who makes them."

"This type of work is done by artists called medical illustrators," replied his dad. "They combine their knowledge of science, the human body, and art to help people understand complex scientific information. Medical illustrators are specially trained scientific illustrators."

"Wow! That sounds like something I'd like to do," said Carlos. "Imagine teaching science with art!"

Scientific illustrators help us understand animals from the past.

Scientific illustration is a unique and creative way to demonstrate the workings of nature. Illustrations help explain our world, from the tiniest molecules and **microbes**, to humans and plants, to extinct dinosaurs. Scientific illustration is extremely valuable. It can show the qualities of subjects that are difficult to explain in words, such as anatomy, shape, and complicated processes. Like the old saying, a picture is worth a thousand words!

Scientific illustrators blend an understanding of

science with artistic skills to create accurate and detailed work. Their illustrations can be found in textbooks, nature guides, museum exhibits, scientific magazines, Web sites, and many other places. Illustrators work in different techniques and mediums, such as pen and ink, watercolor, charcoal, or oils. Many artists use cutting-edge computer graphics programs and digital techniques. Some scientific illustrators build **three-dimensional** (3-D) models and sculptures in clay, wax, or other materials.

THINK ABOUT SCIENCE

If a career as a scientific or medical illustrator sounds appealing, it's not too early to get on the path toward success. In middle school and high school, take as many science courses as you can. Try to focus on life sciences, which involve the study of all living organisms. Courses in human anatomy, biology, botany (study of plants), zoology (study of animals), cell biology, and genetics will give you a solid foundation to build upon.

One of the most exciting and challenging forms of scientific illustration is medical illustration. Medical illustrators are artists who work in the field of medicine. They are specially trained in medicine and science. These talented artists create representations of medical information, such as drawings of muscles, bones, or surgical procedures. Doctors, students, medical patients, and even lawyers use medical illustrations to better understand **biological** data.

The development of medical illustration dates back hundreds of years. Over time, medical illustrators have provided us with an increasingly more detailed and more accurate view of the human body.

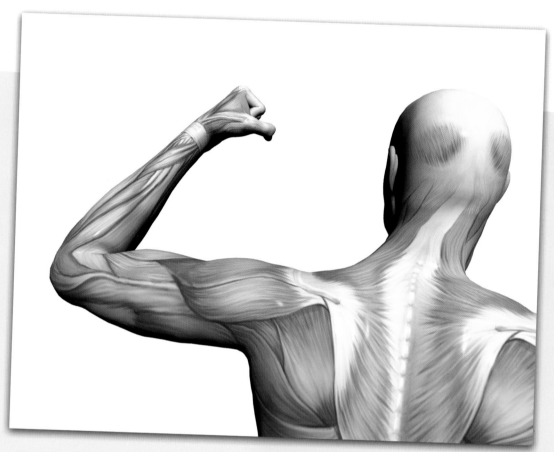

Drawings like this of muscles in the human body were created by a medical illustrator.

CHAPTER 2

PIONEERS OF MEDICAL ILLUSTRATION

Years ago, an amazing drawing was discovered in a prehistoric cave in Spain. The rock drawing showed a **mammoth** with a leaf-shaped dark area where the heart should be. Many researchers believe the drawing— estimated to be 17,000 years old—is the world's first anatomical illustration. Thousands of years later, the ancient Egyptians, Greeks, Romans, Chinese, and others created medical illustrations on stone, ceramic, and other materials. However, the knowledge of anatomy in early civilizations was limited because **dissection** of the

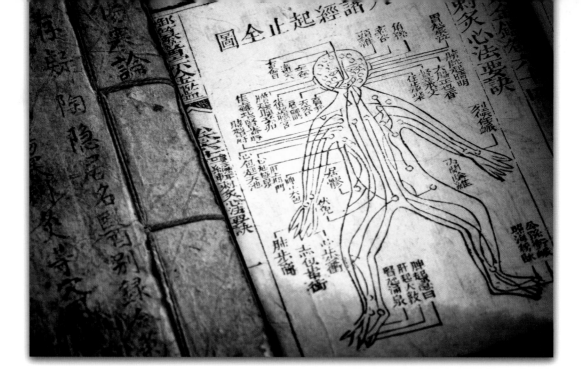

Early illustrations of the human body look much different than today's illustration.

human body was not allowed. Therefore, many of these illustrations were inaccurate. They merely show what the artist thought the internal organs looked like, not how they actually looked.

In the 15th and 16th centuries, artists began creating more realistic art of the human body. Famous artists da Vinci and Michelangelo may have dissected human bodies in a quest to learn more about humans' internal systems and processes. Some artists and physicians worked together to create anatomically accurate illustrations. The drawings

Biological illustrators may begin sketching a project with paper and pencil and then transfer the work to a computer.

and paintings they created led to new biological discoveries and increased medical knowledge.

The first complete written and visual description of the human body was *De Humani Corporis Fabrica* (*On the Fabric of the Human Body*), written by Andreas Vesalius in 1543. The book contains more than 600 illustrations based on dissections that Vesalius performed. Today, illustrations from the book are still used to teach art students the difficult task of medical illustration.

The profession of medical illustrator is relatively young. In the 1890s, Max Brödel (1870–1941), a German artist who immigrated to the United States, began to illustrate for doctors at the Johns Hopkins School of Medicine in Baltimore, Maryland. Brödel created new techniques of anatomical drawing, and in 1911 he established at Johns Hopkins the first school of medical illustration in the United States. The school continues to provide professional illustrators with an outstanding scientific background as well as an artistic one.

THINK ABOUT TECHNOLOGY

Modern advances in computer graphics and imaging are creating new opportunities for medical illustrators. The workings of cells too small to be seen even by the most sophisticated microscopes can now be brought to life through computer animations. Technologies such as the Internet and wireless networks enable scientific information to be widely available to nearly everybody.

Frank Netter (1906–1991), born in New York City, was another significant contributor to the field of medical illustration. Netter's family disapproved of his career as an artist, so he went to medical school and began practicing medicine. The economic hardships of the Great Depression of the 1930s, however, forced him to turn to medical art to earn a living. He began working for drug companies. Netter went on to produce nearly 4,000 illustrations that appeared in books, medical magazines and journals, and other publications. Nicknamed the Medical Michelangelo, Netter also published a multivolume atlas of human anatomy, a milestone in the field of medical illustration.

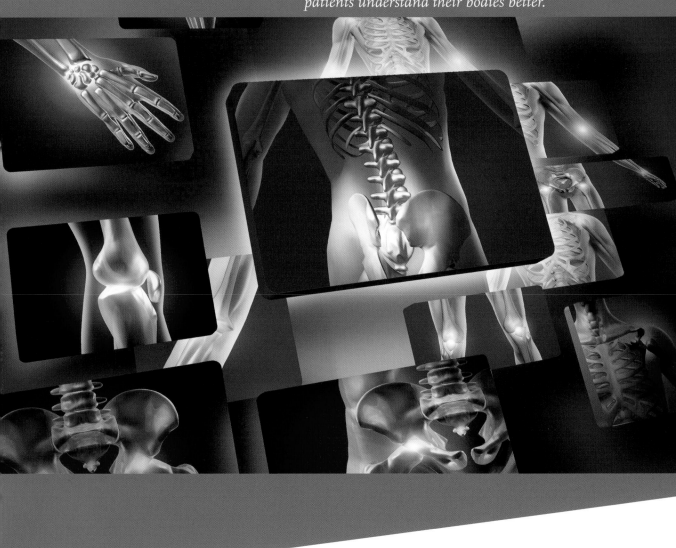

Doctors use medical illustrations to help patients understand their bodies better.

The Role of a Medical Illustrator

Medical illustrators are visual problem solvers. Educated in medicine and art techniques, they have the right skills to communicate complex information to a broad range of audiences. Medical illustrators rarely work alone. They frequently team up with physicians, scientists, and other professional specialists. Their work encourages learning and documents scientific advances and discoveries.

A medical illustrator can apply his or her expertise to a wide variety of tasks. Some illustrators create striking images for textbooks and other materials used by doctors

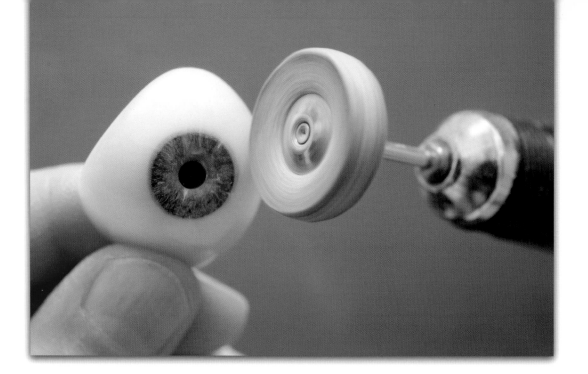

A medical illustrator's job may include building artificial body parts.

and students. They may illustrate or create animations to show the correct sequence of steps during complex, lifesaving operations. At other times, they may create drawings of healthy and diseased body parts to show the effects of illness. In some cases, they create illustrations that appear in brochures and pamphlets read by patients trying to understand their own personal medical conditions. Some illustrators might even build artificial body parts, such as eyes or ears, for patients who require them.

There is a rapidly expanding need for Web-based interactive learning programs.

In recent years, the work of medical illustrators has been used to educate people in several unique places. In New York City, students at the New York University School of Medicine use medical illustrations and animations to perform dissections on "**virtual**" dead bodies. In Washington, D.C., the Smithsonian used animation to go along with an exhibit called *Genes and Jazz*. Animated surgeries and other medical procedures are frequently shown on television programs such as *The Doctors* and on Web sites such as www.youtube.com.

The Internet and wireless technology give professionals and the public greater access to health care information. To meet the growing demand for information, medical illustrators provide accurate and visually exciting material.

THINK ABOUT ENGINEERING

Biomedical engineering is a field that combines the design and problem-solving skills of engineering with biological and medical sciences. Working with physicians and engineers, medical illustrators often help design artificial body parts, such as arms, legs, and ears. These designs improve the lives of people who need replacements for body parts that have been damaged by injury or disease.

CHAPTER 4

Tools of the Trade

The Association of Medical Illustrators (AMI) estimates that there are about 2,000 professionally trained medical illustrators in the world. Slightly more than 1,200 illustrators practice in all of North America. These statistics tell us that medical illustration is a relatively exclusive field in which only a few specialized artists practice. However, don't let the numbers discourage you from considering medical illustration as a career. It's an especially rewarding occupation, one that makes a real difference in people's lives.

Medical illustrators often have experience in many different kinds of art.

You'll need to enjoy and have abilities in both art and science, particularly biology and medicine, to become a medical illustrator. Future medical illustrators need to be skilled in a wide range of art techniques and methods. This includes traditional drawing and painting techniques, 3-D sculpting, and state-of-the-art computer graphics skills.

Students interested in medical illustration should enjoy and be capable of working both alone and as part of a team. Illustrators frequently meet and share ideas with physicians, clients, and other professionals throughout a

Medical illustrators review project details with doctors throughout the illustration process.

project. Solid communication skills, both writing and verbal, are a huge plus. Research and computer skills are also valuable.

Interestingly, law firms often use medical illustrators. They may hire illustrators to reconstruct crime scenes. At other times, illustrators might prepare drawings and graphics to support statements made by witnesses during a trial. Sometimes a medical illustrator may even use photos to re-create facial features of an unrecognizable dead person.

Earnings vary based on the experience of the illustrator, the type of work performed, and the region or country where he or she lives. AMI reports that the median annual salary for an illustrator working for a business is roughly $65,000. But an illustrator can earn up to $150,000 annually. The median salary is the wage that half the workers earn more than and half earn less than. The median income for a self-employed medical illustrator is about $80,000, but earnings can be as high as $250,000 per year.

THINK ABOUT ART

A career in medical illustration is built on a strong foundation in drawing and design. At the college level, medical illustration students take courses that include color theory, anatomic illustration, 3-D modeling, photography, and surgical illustration. Some schools require students to take other courses that broaden their understanding of the historical development of art. These courses might include Western art and architecture, Latin American art, Renaissance art, and 20th-century art.

CHAPTER 5

A Career as a Medical Illustrator

Becoming a medical illustrator requires the right planning, training, and education. Most medical illustrators have a master's degree from an **accredited** two-year graduate program. The Commission on Accreditation of Allied Health Education Programs grants accreditation to deserving programs. There are presently three accredited medical illustration programs in the United States and one in Canada. Competition to get into a program is strong. Each program usually accepts a maximum of 16 or even fewer students each year.

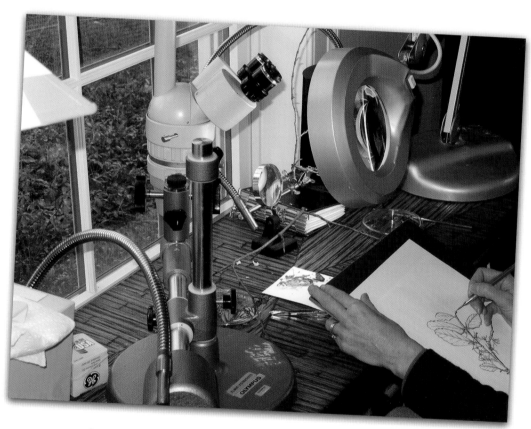

One step along the way to becoming a medical illustrator is
to earn a degree related to fine art and to biological science.

A class in human anatomy is required for a medical illustration graduate degree.

To qualify for a graduate program, students should have a bachelor's degree with a fine arts major and a biological science minor, or a science major with a fine arts minor. By the time you apply for a graduate program, you should have a solid **portfolio** of your artwork. Your portfolio will be reviewed by the program's directors.

Graduate medical illustration programs include science courses in many areas, including anatomy, surgery, **pathology**, and **physiology**. Art classes include surgical illustration, 3-D modeling and Web

design, and traditional drawing and computer techniques. Programs often offer instruction in specialty areas such as advanced video graphics and patient prosthetics, or artificial body parts. Most programs require a master's thesis for completion of the degree.

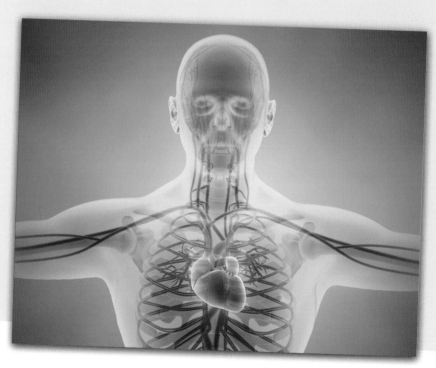

Using a computer to create digital images like this is common for a medical illustrator.

Knowing how to create up-to-date digital art is an important skill for a medical illustrator.

Not all employers require job candidates to have a master's degree, and you probably wouldn't need one if you choose to be self-employed. Future medical illustrators may earn bachelor's degrees in premedical illustration or medical illustration from a four-year college or university. In these programs, students take courses that include drawing fundamentals; human and animal biology; digital drawing; and 3-D illustration.

The future looks bright for medical illustrators. The

U.S. Bureau of Labor Statistics claims that illustrators—especially those with up-to-date skills in computer graphics and animation—will find good employment opportunities in the next decade. This is due to the rapid growth of the health care field and new medical advancements and discoveries. Medical illustrators will be called upon to communicate these developments visually.

Are you up to the challenge?

THINK ABOUT MATH

A medical illustrator's work must be accurate. Illustrations showing the comparative size of internal organs, for example, must be precise. Step-by-step animations showing the correct way a surgery must be performed need to be error-free and easy to understand. Medical illustrators rely on math skills to make sure their measurements of biological structures are accurate. Undergraduate courses in medical illustration often include algebra and trigonometry, calculus and geometry, and some form of statistics.

THINK ABOUT IT

How do medical illustrators help communicate complex medical and scientific information?

How are medical illustrators used during court cases?

After reading this book, how do you think medical illustration and animation help improve people's lives or even save lives?

LEARN MORE

FURTHER READING

Ames, Lee J. *Draw the Draw 50 Way*. New York: Watson-Guptill Publications, 2012.

Ferguson's Careers in Focus: Art. New York: Ferguson, 2008.

Rohlander, Nathan. *Drawing: The Figure*. Irvine, CA: Walter Foster, 2011.

Walker, Richard, with Nick Abadzis (illustrator). *Dr. Frankenstein's Human Body Book: The Monstrous Truth About How Your Body Works*. New York: DK Publishing, 2008.

WEB SITES

Association of Medical Illustrators
www.ami.org/index.php/medical-illustration/enter-the-profession/careers
Learn more about the skills and training required to be a medical illustrator, as well as the career opportunities in this exciting field.

Science Magazine—I Am a Medical Illustrator
http://sciencecareers.sciencemag.org/career_magazine/previous_issues
/articles/2002_05_24/nodoi.6994029340208744503
Read a revealing interview with a professional medical illustrator.

U.S. National Library of Medicine—Medical Illustration: Art in Medical Education
www.ncbi.nlm.nih.gov/pmc/articles/PMC3221200
Read about the history of medical illustration, from prehistoric times to the present.

GLOSSARY

accredited (uh-KRED-uh-ted) approved as having met certain standards

anatomy (uh-NAT-uh-mee) the structure of a living thing, such as a human or an animal

animations (an-uh-MAY-shuhnz) movies made by using drawings, pictures, or computer graphics

biological (bye-uh-LAH-ji-kuhl) of or relating to the study of life and all living things

circulatory system (SUR-kyuh-luh-tor-ee SIS-tuhm) the group of organs that pump blood through the body, including the heart, veins, and arteries

dissection (di-SEKT-shuhn) the cutting apart of a human or animal body so as to examine it

mammoth (MAM-uhth) an extinct animal that looked like a large elephant, with long, curved tusks and shaggy hair

microbes (MYE-krohbz) extremely small living things, especially ones that cause disease

pathology (pa-THOL-uh-jee) the scientific and medical study of disease, its causes, its processes, and its effects

portfolio (port-FO-lee-oh) a bound book or folder with a set of pictures that have been compiled over a period of time that show progress

physiology (fiz-ee-AHL-uh-jee) the scientific study of the activities and processes essential to living organisms

three-dimensional (THREE duh-MEN-shuh-nuhl) having or seeming to have depth, or the three dimensions of length, width, and height

virtual (VUR-choo-uhl) made to seem like the real thing, but consisting mainly of sound and images

INDEX